Swati Sengupta is an author and journalist. Her books include *Out of War* (Speaking Tiger Books, 2016), *Guns on My Red Earth* (Rupa, 2013), *Half the Field Is Mine* (Scholastic, 2014), *The Talking Bird* (Tulika Books, 2014) and *A Tea Garden Party* (Pratham Books, 2021). She translated *Murder in the City* (Speaking Tiger Books, 2018) from Bengali to English. Swati runs a workshop series on gender for young adults. She studied English at Jadavpur University and lives in Kolkata.

Also in the series by Swati Sengupta:

Jhalkari Bai: The Braveheart Warrior

Milkha Singh: The Runner Who Could Fly

Birsa Munda: The Great Revolutionary Leader

Savitribai Phule: The Fearless Reformer

Arati Saha: The Swimmer Who Wouldn't Give Up

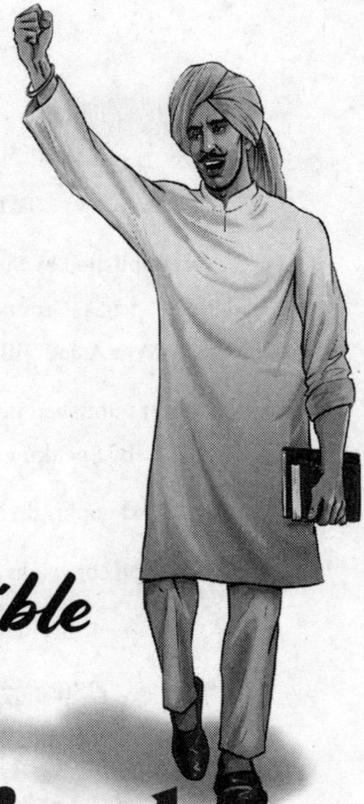

The Incredible Life of
Bhagat Singh
The Indomitable Freedom Fighter

Swati Sengupta

Illustrations by Sridatri Tagore

talking CUB
An Imprint of Speaking Tiger Books

TALKING CUB

Published by Speaking Tiger Books LLP
125A, Ground Floor, Shahpur Jat,
Near Asiad Village, New Delhi 110 049

First published in paperback in Talking Cub
by Speaking Tiger Books in 2023

ISBN: 978-93-5447-695-2

eISBN: 978-93-5447-696-9

10 9 8 7 6 5 4 3 2 1

Typeset in Georgia by Jojy Philip
Printed at HT Media Ltd, Greater Noida

To A, for being a bit like Bhagat,
adopting atheism and a strong political
ideology at such a young age

Chapter One

A three-year-old boy ran unsteadily into the fields. He was dressed in a shirt and khaki shorts, and his long, silky hair was tied up in a tiny bun. He threw himself to the ground and started digging with his bare hands. What fun this was! His father, Kishan Singh, watched him fondly from a distance.

The tracts of lush fields were at Banga village, Lyallpur, Punjab, and the time was 1910. This tranquil and serene village was in western Punjab, 150 kilometres from Lahore.

But no place was really peaceful anywhere in the country.

The British had been in India for over a hundred years now. A few years earlier—in 1905—the first partition of Bengal had taken place. A new province of Eastern Bengal was created with its capital at Dacca. Indians had protested against this, and at mass rallies the rebellious cry of 'Vande Mataram' (Hail to Thee, Mother) had rent the air. The boycotting and burning of British-made goods had started in different parts of the country. In 1906, in the Calcutta session of the Congress, a demand for Swaraj, or self-rule, had been made. Indians were awakening to the idea of freedom—that the country had to be governed by Indians, not the British. But how would Indians achieve this?

By militant, violent means, or through dialogue and discussions? Which path would the country choose eventually?

Kishan Singh, the little boy's father, was walking with Mehta Anand Kishore. As the two men came closer to the boy, they saw the three-year-old was engrossed in something. His clothes were grubby and his face smeared with dirt and mud. He was digging the ground, and had made several holes already.

'What *are* you doing?' asked Kishan Singh lovingly of his son, Bhagat. There was no answer from the busy little boy. Kishan Singh lowered his head, held his cheek against little Bhagat's, and asked him again.

Now the boy spoke, with a resolve that was nothing like that of a three year old: 'I am sowing guns, so that when they sprout, we will be able to get rid of the British.'

Kishan Singh and Mehta Anand Kishore exchanged glances. At that moment they knew that it would be impossible to keep the child away from the passion and intensity of nationalism. After all, everyone in the family always discussed how to achieve freedom from British rule. How could little Bhagat not be a part of it?

Little did they know that Bhagat Singh would go on to be one of the country's greatest freedom fighters. His distinctive thoughts, ideology,

strength of character, resolve and fearlessness would set him apart and he would be remembered fondly and with great respect forever.

~

The family's ancestral home was in Khatkar Kalan near Jalandhar. In the 1840s, Bhagat's great grandfather Fateh Singh had fought against the British in Maharaja Ranjit Singh's army in the Anglo-Sikh war. As a fallout, a part of the family's land and property was seized by the British East India Company.

In the early 1900s, the family moved from Khatkar Kalan to Lyallpur when they were allotted land there. The British had dug canals in this region for the formation of colonies where agriculture could be commercialized. Bhagat

Singh's family got their land in Chak No. 105 in Lyallpur.

Fateh Singh's son, Sardar Arjan Singh, was an Arya Samajist—a follower of the Arya Samaj. The Samaj promoted values based on the belief in and the authority of the Vedas. Arjan Singh always lent a helping hand to those in need, especially during natural disasters.

Arjan Singh had three sons—Kishan, Ajit and Swaran. Ajit Singh was a revolutionary thinker. He studied in Anglo-Sanskrit High School in Jalandhar, the Dayanand Anglo-Vedic College, Lahore, and while studying at Bareilly College, he started working for the poor and against the British regime. During famines, he and his elder brother Kishan worked among the poor in various parts of the country, including in Barar, Ahmedabad, Srinagar and Kangla.

In 1907, Ajit Singh was arrested for leading a peasants' agitation, and deported to Myanmar's Mandalay Jail. After his release, he attended the Surat session of the Congress and in 1907, formed a revolutionary organization called the Bharat Mata Society, in which freedom fighter Lala Lajpat Rai was also involved. Later, Singh launched the Bharat Mata Book Agency, that published anti-government literature. He worked closely with many revolutionaries. In 1909, Ajit Singh along with freedom fighter Sufi Amba Prasad fled to Iran.

Bhagat Singh was born on 28 September 1907, to Kishan Singh and Vidyawati. He spent most of his childhood in the company of his grandfather Arjan Singh, and as a result Bhagat was greatly influenced by his spirit of generosity. Though Bhagat was only two years old when his uncle Ajit Singh had left the country, he knew the stories of how his uncle had fought against the British and worked for the poor. All this had a huge influence on the young mind.

Bhagat's father Kishan Singh was a Congress leader and had been in jail several times. Swarn Singh, Kishan Singh's other brother, had been in jail too, where he had contracted tuberculosis and died shortly after his release. Every day, the little boy heard conversations in the family on India's freedom movement.

Bhagat was the second of Kishan Singh and Vidyawati's nine children. The other five sons were Jagat, Kulbir, Kultar, Ranbir and Rajinder. The girls were Amar, Prakash and Shakuntla.

In such a family, how could Bhagat stay away from the spirit of nationalism?

Chapter Two

Vidyawati called out, 'Rotis! They are warm and I want both of you to come right away.' She put dal in bowls and rolled the rotis. She was calling her sons Jagat and Bhagat. 'So much of work is left, where are you?'

The two boys came running after some time.

'Show me your hands. Are they clean?' she asked.

The boys smiled mischievously. Jagat showed his hands, but Bhagat wouldn't.

'Why not?' she asked in mock anger. He tried

to push something into his pocket, but it fell on the floor with a thud.

'There! I knew it!' Vidyawati said. Bhagat picked up the book that had fallen on the floor and tried pushing it into the pocket of his kurta again. But the pocket was torn. Bhagat always carried books with him and would shove them into small pockets, and when they wouldn't fit, the seams of his clothes would come off!

'This child is always putting books into his pockets and tearing them. How many times should I stitch them for you, child?' his mother asked, serving hot rotis on the plates. But inside, she was bursting with happiness and pride that Bhagat was always reading. She knew that the boy would do something outstanding one day.

Jagat was their eldest child. Bhagat was the second born. During the summer months, little Jagat and Bhagat visited the family's ancestral home at Khatkar Kalan, where they would spend the days with grandfather Arjan Singh. There would be peals of laughter as the two boys ran around playing in the fields, enjoying themselves. But in 1916, a wave of sorrow swept through their lives. Jagat died from a flu. He was just eleven. The death was so sudden and unexpected, the family was devastated.

Kishan Singh got some solace in prayers. He encouraged Bhagat, too, to offer prayers daily. But for Bhagat, books offered the escape from the sadness. They took him to far-off lands, they offered him interesting questions and arguments, he came upon new philosophies and ideologies.

All this while, Bhagat was in a school in Lyallapur. Soon, he started going to Dayanand Anglo-Vedic High School in Lahore, an Arya Samajist school.

As a young boy, Bhagat Singh was very aware of what was happening in the country and all around him. He was a brutal critic of senior political leaders, arguing with his father Kishan Singh, agreeing or disagreeing on policies and decisions. Bhagat had a mind of his own from a very early age.

It so happened that some events occurring then would bring sweeping changes in his life. One such took place in Jallianwala Bagh.

~

On 13 April 1919, hundreds of Indians—women, men and children—had gathered at Jallianwala Bagh in Amritsar, Punjab, for a peaceful protest against the British government's imposition of the Rowlatt Act and the arrest of some Indian activists.

> The Anarchical and Revolutionary Crimes Act of 1919—also known as the Rowlatt Act—was a legislation passed by the Imperial Legislative Council, the legislature of British India. This enabled the government to imprison suspects without trial and arrest anyone without offering any reason.

It was brought in on the basis of a report by Justice Sidney Rowlatt's commission of 1918. Nationalist Indians felt that the Act was passed to curb the revolutionary activities against the colonial government. It empowered the British government to arrest anyone suspected of engaging in 'terrorist' activities. Indians resisted the legislature, and Gandhiji called for a satyagraha against the Act. Eventually in 1922 it was repealed along with many other Acts.

As the people gathered there were listening to the speeches, British officer Brigadier General R.E.H. Dyer reached the venue with the British Indian Army. The sudden intrusion didn't scare anyone—British officers often ended such meetings forcibly. They hoped Dyer would leave.

But General Dyer did something horrific. He ordered the entry and exit points into Jallianwala Bagh be closed. He lined up his troops, and barked out an order. The troops fired into the crowd. Bullets rained on the unarmed, peaceful gathering. Screams for help filled the air as people ran in desperation, looking for an exit, but the gates were locked. No one—neither the elderly nor the children—was spared. They tried to scale the walls, but the troops fired at them. People dropped dead on the ground. General Dyer stood there, watching the bloodbath. Bodies lay piled upon each other. Once it stopped, streams of blood flowed and drenched the ground. According to the British, around 400 people were killed, though Indian historians say that the number was 1,000, with over 1,200 injured. It was a brutal act of violence.

Bhagat Singh was eleven years old when the Jallianwala Bagh massacre took place. Some days later, he went to Amritsar with his family.

As he reached the ground, young Bhagat was choked with emotion. Tears in eyes, he bent down and scooped up a handful of soil. He held the soil against his forehead in an act of respect. Heart heavy with sorrow, he kept the soil in a jar at home. It would be a constant reminder to him of the brutality with which the British rulers had killed his fellow Indians. He wouldn't let himself forget the cries of those innocent people.

As he lay in bed that night, he realized that even the twinkling stars above and the cool breeze caressing his cheeks felt suffocating. How to end this slavery, Bhagat wondered.

Can young people do anything to bring about significant change? The grave injustice of Jallianwala Bagh massacre made Bhagat think that he should not remain a passive observer. 'I must do something about it,' he told himself.

~

Yet another major influence on the young Bhagat was the Ghadar movement. It was formed in 1913 by expatriate Punjabis in the United States and Canada. Its goal was to overthrow the British colonial rule in India. The Ghadar movement planned to print pamphlets, send arms and volunteers who would carry out acts of rebellion. In fact, the movement is considered to be one of the first revolutionary struggles for India's freedom. The courage and sacrifices and the feeling of nationalism of the Ghadarites attracted Bhagat Singh to the movement and its leaders.

When World War I broke out in 1914, the Ghadarites considered it a good opportunity to return to India to launch a war against British rule. Many started moving to India in ships, but within some time, most of its leaders faced imprisonment or life transportation. Forty-six convicts were executed, the youngest of them being Kartar Singh Sarabha. He was only nineteen years old when he was hanged in November 1915. Bhagat Singh had heard the stories of Ghadarites as a child. In fact, some were known to have visited his father and uncles. Bhagat considered Sarabha a hero and often carried his photograph.

By the time Bhagat was a teenager—fourteen or fifteen years old—he had a deep understanding of politics. He was beginning to have his own opinions on the Indian freedom movement and the path that Indians should take.

Chapter Three

In 1919, the British government had passed the Rowlatt Act, despite stiff opposition from Indians. Added to this, the Jallianwala Bagh massacre was a huge setback for the Indians who had hoped India's Independence would come soon.

Around this time, Mohandas Karamchand Gandhi had returned from South Africa in 1915, and swept across the country, infusing fresh ideas. Gandhi's influence on the people was massive, and he was loved and respected. After a call for Rowlatt satyagaraha in 1919 to oppose the Rowlatt Act, he now gave a call for a Non-cooperation movement with a demand to grant India self-rule or Swaraj. Millions of Indians across the country took to the streets. It was a non-violent movement involving boycotting government services, educational institutions, foreign-made goods and even paying taxes. The Congress took it up on a large scale from December 1920.

But an incident in Chauri Chaura of Gorakhpur in the United Provinces changed everything. On 4 February 1922, when a large group of protestors participating in the Non-cooperation movement clashed with the police, the latter opened fire. In retaliation, the protestors set fire to a police station, killing all those inside. The casualty: three civilians and twenty-three policemen. The fallout? Mahatma Gandhi called off the Non-cooperation movement.

The teenager Bhagat was a more mature thinker now, argumentative, logical and assertive. He could not agree with the decision taken by Gandhiji to call off the Non-cooperation movement.

'This is not right,' Bhagat said to his father.

'What?' asked Kishan Singh.

'The Non-cooperation movement should not have been called off. It was important to continue with it for our freedom,' Bhagat said.

'But Gandhiji had to take a call after the Chauri Chaura incident. The Non-cooperation movement was meant to be non-violent. Chauri

Chaura was against its principles,' Kishan Singh said.

'Did he seek others' opinions before making the announcement? Does he know what the youth think? Do we know why Chauri Chaura turned violent? Can the British continue with their violent acts on Indians while we stick to our promises of non-violence?' Bhagat asked, cheeks flushed with emotion. 'This will give out a bad signal to the British. They will think of us as cowards. Why should *we* back out when *they* have wronged us?'

A feeling of sorrow swept over Kishan Singh as he listened to his son. Would such strong opinions be good or bad for Bhagat? Where would he end up with such intense feelings?

Kishan Singh patted his son's shoulder and

said: 'I am sure, if we think hard, some solution will soon come into view.' But deep inside, he felt worried for Bhagat.

~

After finishing school, Bhagat joined National College, Lahore, set up by Lala Lajpat Rai in 1921 in Bradlaugh Hall. Bhagat was among the first to join the college, which was started as an alternative to the British education system. The aim was to make students politically aware, focused on independent thinking, and the students were encouraged to read on politics, history and economics. They even learned about freedom movements and revolutions in other parts of the world.

Bradlaugh Hall itself was a symbol of nationalism. It was built by the Indian National Congress in 1900, as a place to organize its political events. In 1893, at the annual session in Lahore, it was decided to build such a place through fundraising. The hall was named after British Parliamentarian Charles Bradlaugh, who visited India in 1889 and attended the Congress' fifth annual session. Surendra Nath Banerji, a senior Congress leader, installed a dedication plaque at the inauguration of Bradlaugh Hall on 30 October 1900.

For the young Bhagat Singh and his friends, college meant meeting people from various parts of India. There were hours of debates and discussions at the library, boat rides on River Ravi, watching films, reading books, organizing plays.

Yashpal was one such friend. Bhagat and Yashpal went on long boat rides. They often discussed how the future of the youth of the country was bleak, and that the chains of slavery needed to be broken. They had to free India from the colonizers. Amidst the rippling waters and the distant call of birds, the two young men would think deeply about the future of their nation.

'Let us pledge our life to our country,' Yashpal said once, holding Bhagat's hand.

'I pledge my life to our country,' promised Bhagat.

'And let's go the Dwarka Das Library,' added Bhagat, 'for that is where we will find our path to the country's freedom.' They both laughed at this. 'Come on, let's run to the library now, I must pick up a book,' said Bhagat.

Chapter Four

The Dwarka Das Library of Lahore was established in 1920 by Lala Lajpat Rai as part of the National College. Named after Arya Samaj educationist and Rai's friend, the library was a huge attraction for the young men for many reasons.

When Rai opened the library, he said: 'It will be the first political library in the country in which students of economics and politics will be able to satisfy their appetite.'

There were books here on many political

topics as well as social movements. There were books on Marxism, the Russian Revolution, the Irish Independence movement, and more. Dressed in a long white kurta and loose bottoms, a grey turban on his head, Bhagat was the picture of simplicity as he roamed among the shelves of the library, choosing books to read. The loose end of the turban fell on his shoulder, and he used it to wipe his face often. His moustache was trimmed, but not with a lot of care. He had not shaved his beard for several days. Despite

the mildly scruffy appearance so characteristic of young college-going men, what stood out in this young man was his piercing eyes—one could not escape their intensity. And one could not miss him in a crowd. There were dreams in those eyes, as well as a mix of conviction and curiosity.

Bhagat made a mental note of the books he would borrow the next time. There were so many books to read, though he always spent sleepless nights trying to finish the ones he had borrowed.

'Is there any specific book you are looking for, young man?' asked a man, tapping him on the shoulder.

Startled, Bhagat turned around. A serious-looking man—much older than him—wearing dhoti-kurta, enquired. It was Rajaram Shastri, the librarian. Shastriji himself had been greatly influenced by many books there, and he wanted to help those who came to the library. The library was like a place of worship for him, and he did his job with utmost care. 'There are hundreds of books here on so many subjects...you will find books on socialist literature, on revolution... May I suggest a few titles for you?' Shastriji asked Bhagat. It was not easy to understand the tastes and preferences of readers initially, but Rajaram Shastri always spotted the dedicated readers. And here was a most sparkling star, he noticed when Bhagat Singh visited the library.

At that moment another young man entered the library. He was Sukhdev Thapar. Bhagat Singh and he got talking while deciding which books to read next.

As Bhagat read more, his thoughts kept developing. He now knew a lot about various political philosophies, like anarchism and socialism.

Anarchism is a political philosophy that believes in the liberty of individuals and is against authority and power, especially of the state.

Socialism is a theory that says a community, rather than individuals, should own and manage property and natural resources. It believes that public ownership of property and means of production will lead to an equal society.

As he read books on anarchism and socialism, Bhagat Singh was filled with a delightful excitement. The books nurtured his soul, and were motivating him to work towards a fair and equal society, where power would lie in the hands of the common people.

Over the next few years, Bhagat Singh devoured books on nationalism, socialism, anarchism, and secret underground work. Bhagat Singh was always spotted reading a book. During this time, he often held long discussions at the library with his friends Rajaram Shastri and Sukhdev Thapar. They debated about socialism, the works of Karl Marx, Vladimir Lenin. They discussed the French Revolution, the Irish revolution, and more.

Most importantly, the library would not just remain a reading space. It gradually turned into a place to recruit young revolutionaries. Shastri keenly followed the interests of the students visiting the library and informed Bhagat and

Sukhdev if someone showed interest in books on socialism, revolution, anarchism and so on. Very soon, the library came under police surveillance.

Apart from Sukhdev and Bhagat Singh, many other students joined their sessions—Bhagwati Charan Vohra, Ehsan Elahi, Durgadas Khanna and Yashpal, among others.

During this time, Bhagat acted in plays like *Samrat Chandragupta* and *Rana Pratap*. He was also fond of films. Whenever his eyes caught advertisements in newspapers on the release of a film, he would rush to the theatre halls with his friends, provided they had the money to buy tickets.

Bhagat and his friends went to the Excelsior Theatre in Lahore to watch the silent film, *Uncle Tom's Cabin*, based on Harriet Beecher Stowe's novel of the same name. After watching it, Bhagat delivered a passionate speech on it. 'It is essential for all revolutionaries to watch the film,' he said.

Some books Bhagat Singh read and was inspired by are:

Maxim Gorky's *Mother*

Victor Hugo's *Ninety-Three* and *Les Miserables*

Mikhail Bakunin's *God and the State*

A collection of essays by Emma Goldman titled *Anarchism and Other Essays*

Charles Dickens' *A Tale of Two Cities*

The works of Upton Sinclair

Jaakoff Prelooker's *Heroes and Heroines of Russia*

Some films he watched and enjoyed were:

Uncle Tom's Cabin

Wildcat of Bombay

Wings

Wings was the first film to win an Oscar—the Academy Award for Outstanding Picture. The lead role in *Wildcat of Bombay* was played by Ruby Myers (whose screen name was Sulochana) where she played eight different roles that included Indian men and British spies.

Chapter Five

Kishan Singh and his wife were beginning to worry about their son. It was clear to them by now that he was no ordinary college-going student. Kishan Singh had himself been imprisoned, his brother Ajit had to leave the country and another brother Swarn had died after being released from prison. He could not bear to think that Bhagat would not experience the joys of an ordinary life involving friends and family.

'The lives of freedom fighters involve enormous sacrifices. I don't want my child to go through the pain,' Vidyawati said, weeping. Kishan Singh consoled his wife, but he was just as perturbed.

In order to lead Bhagat away from the harsh life of a revolutionary, Kishan Singh and his wife made a plan. They decided to get Bhagat married, as they felt that it would be the only 'solution' to keep him away from revolutionary activities. It was 1923, and Bhagat was just sixteen years old at that time.

Bhagat did not react at first. He was mature beyond his years. 'They will be hurt if I turn down their proposal immediately. I know why they are planning it,' he told himself. 'They want to tie me down to family life so that the home becomes my focus instead of my country.'

The young man believed that devoting his

life to the country was his destiny. 'Moreover, why should I ruin the life of another person by involving her in my life? Especially when I cannot think of a life that is not dedicated to my country...' At that moment, the faces of Hukam Kaur and Harnam Kaur came into his mind. Hukam was Swarn Singh's widow and Harnam was wife of Ajit Singh, who was living in exile.

Bhagat Singh was a sensitive young man. He had seen the plight of his two aunts who had lived without their husbands for years. Finally, Bhagat decided what he would do. He left a letter for his father:

> *Dear Father, I apologize for not fulfilling your wishes... My life has been dedicated to the service of this country and the comforts and worldly desires are not meant for me.*

The hopes and wishes of the parents were dashed. 'We tried our best,' sighed Kishan Singh, trying to console his wife, who wept bitterly.

~

Bhagat Singh left for Kanpur. It was the beginning of a new journey for him, from now on he would be the master of his own choices and decisions.

His teacher from National College, Jai Chander Vidyalankar, gave Bhagat a letter of introduction to Congress leader of the United Provinces Ganesh Shankar Vidyarthi. Vidyarthi was a leading editor and journalist, whose Hindi publication, *Pratap*, had come under the scrutiny of the British administration.

Pratap started as a weekly magazine, and then became a daily newspaper. Vidyarthi was its editor since 1913. *Pratap* made its readers aware of their rights as Indians. It published articles that told its readers to not get divided by caste and religious differences. Many newspapers and magazines run by Indians were critical of the British administration, and it was a tough job for those like Vidyarthi to run a publication. The office of *Pratap* was raided many times and in 1915, it was fined Rs 1,000 for publishing anti-British articles. It remained closed for about a year, and started publishing again from July 1918.

Vidyarthi was impressed by the young Bhagat Singh. Conviction and courage were written large on his face. His eyes were full of dreams and he was ready to take on the world to bring justice to the ordinary people of his country.

Vidyarthi asked Bhagat to write for *Pratap.* The voracious reader soon became a writer.

'Let Balwant Singh be my pen name,' Bhagat said. 'Let no one know the real author of these articles.' Sometimes he also wrote under the pen name 'Vidrohi' or 'B.S. Sindhu'. In fact, during these uncertain times when the British government kept a close watch, many revolutionaries chose to write under pen names. After all, their main purpose in writing was to influence ordinary people across the country, and inspire them to join the freedom movement.

When Bhagat Singh started writing in 1923, his thoughts began to blossom into powerful words. Bhagat also wrote for publications like *Matwala*, *Vir Arjun*, *Maharathi*, *Prabha*, *Akali*, *Chand*, *Bande Mataram*, among others. He could write in Punjabi, Urdu and Hindi and occasionally in English. He also wrote for *Kirti*, a reputed Punjabi magazine, from March 1925 to July 1928. He expressed his revolutionary and progressive ideas in these articles. Through these writings, Bhagat Singh influenced and inspired many young men and women, encouraging them to make sacrifices, to take the difficult path and to dream of a free India.

Over the years, he wrote many articles under different pseudonyms. His was a passionate voice calling upon the country's youth to fight for justice. Bhagat praised Kartar Singh Sarabha in many of these articles, and upheld his example for young persons across the country to follow.

Chapter Six

In Kanpur, Bhagat worked as a teacher in a school, wrote for magazines and newspapers, and worked for flood relief. Around this time, he met some Communist leaders like Shaukat Usmani and Muzaffar Ahmed among others in Kanpur and Lahore. Ahmed and Usmani were among the founders of the Communist movement in India. Communist groups were formed in different parts of the country with Ahmed leading in Bengal and Usmani in the United Provinces. Usmani was actively involved with the émigré Communist Party of India, established in Tashkent in 1920. The CPI in India was formed in Kanpur in 1925.

It was in Kanpur that Bhagat met Batukeswar Dutt, whose family was from a village called Oadhi in the Burdwan region of Bengal. Bhagat and Batukeswar became a popular duo in their friends' circles. When Dutt recited poems by the Bengali revolutionary poet Kazi Nazrul Islam, Bhagat tried to learn them. Both read Karl Marx. The city was flooded in 1924 and both volunteered to work during this time as part of

the Tarun Sangh, an organization of the young. They would stand by the Ganga at night holding lanterns to guide anyone trying to reach the shore. Many years later, Bhagat and Batukeswar would meet again in Calcutta and do something momentous together.

After spending some months in Kanpur, writing for *Pratap* under the name Balwant, Bhagat Singh returned to Lahore as his grandmother was unwell. He was promised that the talk of marriage would not be brought up again. He also joined the Hindustan Republican Association (HRA), a revolutionary organization.

Around this time, many young persons had rejected Mahatma Gandhi's path of non-violence and were going down the road of armed revolution, inspired by movements in other countries. These young Indians formed organizations that operated as fitness clubs but were in reality secret organizations that arranged for firearms and ammunition to fight the British.

In 1926, the Naujawan Bharat Sabha (NBS) was formed by Bhagat Singh along with his revolutionary comrades. It followed the youth organizations in Italy inspired by Giuseppe Mazinni and Garibaldi.

Mazinni was a revolutionary and founder of Giovine Italia (Young Italy), a secret organization formed to liberate Italian states from foreign rule. Giuseppe Garibaldi was an Italian patriot and soldier who led the conquest of Sicily and Naples with guerrilla warfare.

Bhagat and his friends were hugely influenced by them. Bhagat Singh was the general secretary of NBS and Bhagwati Charan Vohra was its propaganda secretary. Others included Dhanwantri, Ehsan Elahi, Ram Krishna. Vohra was a close friend of Bhagat. The son of a rich Gujarati, Vohra was part of the same group of friends as Sukhdev and Yashpal. All of them often visited Vohra's Lahore home. Bhagwati Charan was married to Durga Devi when she was just eleven years old.

The NBS focused on popularizing swadeshi goods, simple living, physical fitness and so on. They organized peasants and labourers as they felt that without the involvement of ordinary peasants and labourers, a nation cannot be truly free.

'The strength of the nation lies with the young,' they said. 'We must also set examples on equality—no differences can exist on the basis of caste, class, religion.'

Secularism was its top priority. No wonder then that they even issued leaflets rejecting the gods from different religions and said Karl Marx and Friedrich Engels were the greatest men in the world.

Karl Marx was a German philosopher, born in 1818 in Trier, Prussia. He studied law and philosophy at the University of Berlin and joined a group called Young Hegelians that criticized political establishments of that time. He became a journalist and his critical writings got him expelled by the governments of France, Germany and Belgium.

In 1848, Marx and another German thinker Friedrich Engels published

The Communist Manifesto, that introduced their concept of socialism. In 1867, Marx published the first volume of *Capital* (German: *Das Kapital)* which was about his notions on capitalism and its ill effects. It was a path-breaking publication that has continued to influence generations.

The 1917 Russian Revolution that had overthrown three centuries of tsarist rule, was rooted in Marx's beliefs. The leader of the Russian Revolution—Vladimir Lenin—was deeply influenced by Marxian thoughts.

To join the NBS, one had to sign a pledge to always work for the interest of the nation before that of the community. From the outside, NBS performed various social duties and responsibilities, including charitable work.

However, in reality, it was an underground or secret group of revolutionaries.

The members cooked and ate together, rejecting religious restrictions. These gatherings became a powerful tool to bring together people from different communities.

~

The Naujawan Bharat Sabha not only influenced the young, it also influenced the *very* young.

And so the Bal Bharat Sabha (BBS) started. It was an organization of schoolchildren between the ages of twelve and sixteen. The Bal Student Union (BSU) was also a similar group. The two states with the most number of young freedom fighters were Bengal and Punjab. In fact, 1,192 Indians below fifteen years were convicted of political activities around this time and of these, Punjab had 189 and Bengal 739.

Some of these young people were truly inspiring. Baldev Raj, grandson of Lala Lajpat Rai, was secretary of the BSU. Many young students from schools were active participants of the freedom movement. They took to the streets, shouted slogans and even faced imprisonment. They weren't concerned about themselves. Fighting for the country's freedom was an honour.

When he was just a boy of eleven, Kahan Chand, president of the Amritsar chapter of Bal Bharat Sabha, was sent to three months' rigorous imprisonment. Yash Chand was only ten years old when he was pronounced guilty for assisting the Lahore city unit of the Congress and the NBS.

Bhagat—who always carried a picture of Kartar Singh Sarabha in his pocket—would garland his picture at all the NBS's public meetings. Before every meeting, a picture of Sarabha would be placed on a raised platform in Bradlaugh Hall. Durga Devi, and her sister-in-law Sushila Devi, who were both active in the NBS, cut their fingers and let the drops of blood fall on the white cloth cover of Sarabha's picture. It was their way of making a pledge to work for the country's freedom.

Bhagat Singh would give an impassioned speech at the meetings, telling the audience about the sacrifices of the martyrs and the need to rise and fight the colonizers. He was a great orator, well read and could influence the young.

Chapter Seven

Many important events were taking shape in the early 1920s. Mahatma Gandhi had called off the Non-cooperation movement, which had led to a lot of resentment among the youth. Passionate, and full of conviction, these revolutionaries were greatly influenced by the movements in Italy, Ireland and Russia. They felt the urgent need to take control of the situation in India.

The Hindustan Republic Association (HRA) was formed under this backdrop. Ram Prasad Bismil, Sachindranath Bakshi, Jogesh Chandra

Chatterjee and Sachindranath Sanyal were some of those that set it up in October 1924. The HRA's manifesto, titled *The Revolutionary*, was drafted with great care.

In its manifesto, written in 1925, the HRA said:

'Indian revolutionaries are neither terrorists nor anarchists. They never aim at spreading anarchy in the land, and therefore they can never be properly called anarchists. Terrorism is never their object and they cannot be called terrorists... The present government solely exists because the foreigners have successfully been able to terrorize the Indian people... This official terrorism is surely to be met by counter terrorism. Moreover, the English masters and their hired lackeys can never be allowed to do what they like... Every possible difficulty and resistance must be thrown in their way.'

This is how they decided they would work:

Go for a direct attack.

Hit where it hurts the most: target the money. (This money belonged to Indians but the British had looted it.)

Plan robberies.

HRA's robbery plans were targeted at wealthy landlords and from trains that carried cash collected from various official sources. This money that they looted would be used by the revolutionaries to purchase firearms. After months of planning, Ram Prasad Bismil, Ashfaqullah Khan, Sachindranath Bakshi, Rajendra Lahiri, Chandrashekhar Azad, among others, decided to go ahead with the Kakori train robbery.

On 9 August 1925, as the No.8 Down Train from Shahjahanpur to Lucknow approached Kakori, one of the revolutionaries pulled the chain. The train stopped and he got off with two others. They joined the rest of their group, and together they faced off with the train's guard and looted the cash that was being transported. In this whole process, an Indian—a passenger named Ahmed Ali—got killed accidentally.

The daring train robbery sent alarm bells

ringing throughout the British administration. It was an audacious job and a direct challenge to the government. Knowing that the full might of the police would now be after them, all those involved had to go into hiding. But over a dozen HRA members were arrested within a month. Bismil, Ashfaqullah, Roshan Singh (though he was not involved in the Kakori robbery but a part of HRA) and Rajendra Nath Lahiri were sentenced to be hanged, and others were given long jail terms. Chandrasekhar Azad was the only one among those directly involved who could get away. He escaped to Jhansi, where he stayed hidden. The fallout of the Kakori train robbery was such that with the arrest and execution of the Indian revolutionaries in the region, the HRA was severely crippled.

A big blow was also awaiting Bhagat Singh, though he was not involved in the Kakori robbery.

~

In May 1927, Bhagat Singh was walking in a garden in Lahore, when he was suddenly surrounded by policemen. He was so stunned that he did not even think of trying to escape. And in any case, why should he? He had done nothing.

'Bhagat Singh?' the police asked him.

He neither confirmed, nor denied. 'What for?' was all he said.

'You will know,' they said.

He was calm. What charges would they bring against him? He was taken to a police station, and the following day to the Railway Police lock-up.

A policeman came up to him—an Indian officer—and asked him many questions.

'What do you know about the Kakori robbery?'

'Are the arrested men your associates?'

'Are you a revolutionary?'

'Were you in Lucknow during the Kakori trial?'

'Did you plan to rescue the arrested persons from prison?'

'Did you throw bombs at the crowd during Dussehra?'

After he was bombarded with these questions, the officer finally paused and said: 'You know, Bhagat Singh, if you give any statement or throw any light whatsoever on the activities of the revolutionaries, then you shall not be imprisoned.'

Another pause.

'In fact, not only will you be free, you will be rewarded. Actually, you won't even be produced in court as approver. No one will ever come to know that you shared the information,' the officer added.

Bhagat was flabbergasted. They wanted him to turn on his associates?

Finally, he laughed. 'People who hold ideas like us, don't throw bombs at our innocent people.'

After asking the same questions over and over again, the officer left.

But it was not over yet.

One morning, the Senior Superintendent of the Crime Investigation Department (CID), Newman, came to meet him. He had more in store for Bhagat.

'Let me give you a very sad news,' he began in a stern voice. 'If you do not give us the exact statement we are demanding of you, we'll have to send you to trial for conspiring to wage war. The cases are the Kakori train robbery and the brutal murders on Dussehra,' he said. There was a bomb explosion at a fair in Lahore during Dussehra for which the police were looking for culprits.

Bhagat could not believe his ears!

'Though I am innocent, I am aware that you can do what you so wish,' Bhagat spoke inside his mind, as if he were talking to Newman. Outside, he was mum, and calm as ever.

After Newman had left, the seriousness of the matter began to sink in. Policemen guarding him and serving him food came with advice. 'Young man, you are doomed. Pray to god, for that's the only way you can be saved now,' they told him.

Bhagat Singh did not pray. By then, he had become an atheist–he did not believe in the existence of god.

He was finally released after five weeks, against a bond of Rs 60,000.

Chapter Eight

An important person in Bhagat Singh's life, who was also part of the HRA, was Chandrashekhar Azad. When Azad was fifteen years old, he was caught by the police in Benares in 1921 during a demonstration. Presented before the magistrate, this is how the conversation followed:

'What is your name?'

'Azad.'

'Father's name?'

'Freedom.'

'Where do you live?'

'Prison.'

A furious magistrate ordered fifteen whiplashes. As each lash fell on him, Chandrashekhar Tiwari shouted *'Mahatma Gandhi ki jai'*. From then on, he was called 'Azad'.

After the Non-cooperation movement was withdrawn, a deeply disappointed Chandrashekhar Azad was drawn to the armed revolutionary movement in India. When the HRA started in the United Provinces, Azad became a member of the party. He was a human courier for a while, carrying secret messages. His talent was

soon spotted and he was made part of bigger operations that involved looting big landlords.

He was part of the core team of the Kakori train robbery of 1925, in which everyone directly involved except him was arrested. Azad managed to escape to Jhansi, where he lived patiently for some years, hoping to strike again when the time came.

With nearly the entire HRA team behind bars and facing punishment following the Kakori robbery, it was now time for a new leadership to take over. The responsibility of re-organizing HRA fell on Bhagat Singh and Azad, among others.

A new group of revolutionaries got together. In September 1928, several revolutionaries from north India met at the historic ruins of Feroz

Shah Kotla and changed the name of HRA to Hindustan Socialist Republican Association (HSRA).

Azad was chosen commander-in-chief and head of the military wing, though he was not present at the meeting. The newly formed HSRA wasn't much different in its ideology and functioning from the earlier HRA. HSRA also vowed to discard all religious and caste symbols.

It was from here on that Bhagat Singh came to the forefront of the revolutionary movement along with Chandrashekhar Azad.

~

A landmark event during this time was the formation of the Simon Commission in November

1927. Called the Indian Statutory Commission, it was named after the chairperson Sir John Allsebrook Simon. The commission was going to review government work, check the functioning of various institutions, and offer recommendations for future policies. The members would visit India in 1928, to do this. Indians across the country were enraged. How could a commission to review policies and functioning of institutions in India not have Indians in it? People were out on the streets protesting during the commission's visit in February–March 1928 and October 1928 to April 1929.

On 30 October 1928, when the members reached Lahore, a sea of people met them with black flags and placards that said 'Simon, Go Back'. Leaders at the front were followed by hundreds of ordinary people from all walks of life. From the municipal gate towards the railway station, processions passed through Circular Road and went through Lunda Bazar until it reached Mool Chand Temple Road. About 200 yards from the railway platform, police had placed barbed wires and wooden barricades to stop the protesters. In the first row near the barbed wire stood Lala Lajpat Rai, Maulana Zafar Ali and many other senior leaders.

Despite the slogan shouting by thousands of people, it was a peaceful protest. Suddenly, out of the blue, the police began to strike at the protesters at the order of the Superintendent of Police James A. Scott. He also hit at the crowd with lathis and a knobbed hunter.

Several blows landed on Lala Lajpat Rai during the police lathicharge. Of the many blows that rained on him, one was massive and struck his chest. Other leaders like Raizada Hans Raj, Dr Satya Pal and Dr Muhammad Alam were also beaten up. Some began to bleed, while others lay writhing in pain.

In a statement issued later, Lala Lajpat Rai said: 'Every blow hurled at us this afternoon was a nail in the coffin of the British Empire...I wish to warn the Government that if a violent revolution takes place in this country, the responsibility for bringing it about will fall on such officers as misbehaved themselves today. I would not wonder if the young men go out of our hands and do whatever they choose with the objects of gaining the freedom of their country.'

The incident sent shockwaves across the country. The British government had launched a brutal attack on a senior leader like Lala Lajpat Rai! As messages came pouring in to Rai from leaders across the country, he continued to work. But his health was deteriorating. On November 16, his doctor examined him as he had acute pain.

The next day, Lala Lajpat Rai passed away.

Bhagat Singh and other young revolutionaries like him decided that it was now time to react.

'We won't remain mute spectators anymore,' they said. HSRA leaders decided that the death of Lala Lajpat Rai would be avenged.

Chapter Nine

The British officer behind Lala Lajpat Rai's death must be 'eliminated'—that was how the HSRA decided to avenge the death of Lala Lajpat Rai. Why did these revolutionaries take to violence?

One of the earliest revolutionary organizations was the Atmonnoti Samiti, established in Bengal in 1897. These organizations were formed to attain freedom through armed activities. Prior to World War I, a series of 'political crimes' were committed, followed by continuous government action against the revolutionaries. There were hundreds of arrests or the death sentences of those involved.

The Atmonnoti Samiti later merged with the Anushilan Samiti, founded in 1902 by Satish Chandra Bose and Pramathanath Mitra. After World War I, Indian revolutionaries organized themselves by setting up secret societies, bomb-making factories, and carried out 'political dacoities'. Some say that the approach now was more realistic and programs more concrete. They also made assassination attempts on British officers. Much of this was centred in Assam, Bihar, Bengal with links in United Provinces and Punjab. In 1924, the HRA had been formed in the United Provinces with branches in Benares, Allahabad, Kanpur, Lucknow and so on. Bomb-making was carried out in many Calcutta hideouts, where revolutionaries from U.P. were also trained. Police tracked down and arrested many of these revolutionaries.

Gopinath Saha (who mistakenly killed Ernest Day, a civilian, thinking him to be Calcutta Police Commissioner Charles Tegart) was hanged to death in 1924. Bismil, Rajendranath Lahiri, Ashfaqullah and Roshan Singh were hanged in December 1927 for the Kakori robbery.

And then, Bhagat Singh and Chandrashekhar Azad swung into action. HSRA collaborated with the Bengal revolutionaries and exchanged knowledge on explosives and training.

It was time to strike.

~

The plan was to assassinate Superintendent of Police James A. Scott, the one who had ordered the lathicharge leading to the deadly blows on Lala Lajpat Rai. The HSRA leaders studied maps, chalked down the routes to and from Scott's office, noted his office hours. Sukhdev was the brain behind preparing the blueprint, while Bhagat Singh and Rajguru were chosen to execute it.

Rajguru was a skilled wrestler, a Sanskrit scholar and a brilliant shooter. So perfect was his eye-hand coordination, that he was known in his close circles as the gunman of HSRA.

Sukhdev Thapar, a central committee member and chief of the HSRA's Punjab unit, was an outstanding planner and organizer. He chose the right person for each job and knew the strength of all his HSRA comrades.

On the day of the assassination, it was a long wait for the four assailants. They waited and watched from afar. Their heads were clear, minds sharp as the edges of swords. Around 4 p.m. on 17 December 1928, Assistant Police Superintendent J.P. Saunders, left the District Police Office gate in Lahore along with the Head Constable Chanan Singh.

'That's Scott, our man!' Jai Gopal signalled to Shivaram Rajguru, indicating the British police officer Saunders.

'Are you sure?' Rajguru asked. He wanted to be doubly certain about the target.

Jai Gopal gave the signal for the affirmative.

But it was a mistake.

By then Saunders had started his motorcycle and was driving slowly down the road after exiting the gate. With Jai Gopal's signal, Rajguru took out his revolver and shot at Saunders. The ear-splitting noise reverberated through the air. Saunders lost control and fell. Bhagat Singh darted towards him, automatic pistol in hand. Within moments, he reached the officer and pumped bullets into his body. They had to be sure he was dead. Nothing could be left to chance. Blood trickled to the ground.

Passers-by stood frozen.

Before anyone could react, Rajguru, Jai Gopal and Bhagat Singh fled from the spot. Chanan Singh and Traffic Inspector W.J.G. Fearn gave chase. Chanan Singh came close, and was shot in the thigh.

At first, Bhagat Singh and Rajguru ran out of Court Street into the DAV College compound.

Then they crossed the volleyball ground to the west of Botanical Gardens. They went towards the College Boarding House, and lifting bicycles from the area, rode them onto Dev Samaj Road. Within moments they were out of sight.

They had made their escape.

The lifeless bodies of Saunders and Chanan Singh lay a few yards from each other.

~

It was time to discuss the 'mistake' at their secret hideout. HSRA leaders came to the conclusion that killing Scott or Saunders meant the same as both were senior British police officers and represented the British government in India. HSRA prepared to take responsibility for the killing of Saunders.

The following day, Lahore witnessed something spectacular: walls across the city were pasted with posters announcing the daring act of killing an officer to avenge the death of Lala Lajpat Rai. It was signed by Balraj, the pseudonym of Chandrashekhar Azad.

The Hindustan Socialist Republican Army

Notice

J.P. Saunders is dead!

Lala Lajpat Rai is avenged!

[...]Really it is horrible to imagine that so lowly and violent hand of an ordinary Police Official, J.P. Saunders could ever dare to touch in such an insulting way the body of one so old, so revered and so loved by 300 millions of people of Hindustan and thus cause his death. [...]let the world know

that India still lives; that the blood of youths has not been totally cooled down and that they can still risk their lives, if the honour of their nation is at stake... Do not injure the feeling of a downtrodden and oppressed country... remember that despite 'Arms Act' and strict guards against the smuggling of arms, the revolvers will ever continue to flow in—if not sufficient at present for an armed revolt, then at least sufficient to avenge the national insults... (the) party of young men will ever live to teach a lesson to the haughty rulers... Sorry for the death of a man. But in this man has died the representative of an institution which is so cruel, lowly and so base that it must be abolished. In this man has died an agent of the British authority in India...

Long Live the Revolution!

Sd/ - Balraj

Dated

18th December, 1928

Chapter Ten

At the police station, a report was lodged against two 'unknown gunmen' by an officer. The officer, who was also an eyewitness, recorded that a man he followed was 'five feet five inch', 'had a Hindu face, small moustache, having a slim and strong body, wearing white trouser (pyjama) and grey shirt (kurta), also wearing a small black Christi-like hat'.

HSRA leaders were aware that it wouldn't take long for Bhagat Singh to be identified. He had to escape. But it wasn't possible without the help of close aides. The only one who could pull this off was Durga Bhabhi.

Durga Devi, a teacher at a girls' college in Lahore, was part of the HSRA like her husband Bhagwati Charan Vohra. Earlier in December, Bhagwati Charan had left for Calcutta to attend the annual meeting of the Indian National Congress. It was days after he left that Saunders had been assassinated. 'We must board a train from Lahore station immediately,' Durga Bhabhi suggested.

Bhagat Singh wondered if it would be a good idea. 'Where to?' he asked.

'To Calcutta,' she said. This would help Bhagat escape Lahore and she and her three-year-old son, Sachinanda, could be with Bhagwati Charan at the end of the journey. But there was a look of uncertainty on Bhagat Singh's face. Durga Bhabhi understood the cause of his worry immediately. 'There is five thousand rupees at home,' she said, adding that Bhagwati Charan had left the sum at home in case of emergency.

But Bhagat Singh's scruffy pyjamas, shabby shirt, and overall bedraggled appearance wouldn't work for this journey. He had to dress up as a rich man. Bhagat got into smart clothes, trimmed his moustache, wore an expensive hat.

Dressed as a dandy, he and Durga Bhabhi disguised themselves as a couple along with Sachi, and boarded the first-class coach in a train to Lucknow from Lahore station. Rajguru dressed as their domestic worker. Several things made them melt through strict police surveillance: a rich couple who could afford first-class travel at

that time was unlikely to be revolutionaries. A couple with a child was even less likely to raise suspicion.

As they boarded the train and settled down, Bhagat Singh's heart was pounding—not out of fear, but in the excitement of hoodwinking the British police. No one had guessed that the man who had killed a senior police officer was escaping from right under their noses. That thought brought great satisfaction to the young Bhagat. He had finished an important job.

Not too far away, another sharp young

man, Chandrashekhar Azad, was also escaping Lahore. Azad was in a train too, travelling with Sukhdev's mother and sister. He was disguised as a sadhu, as if he was escorting them on a pilgrimage. Several others who were part of the HSRA fled Lahore similarly.

When Bhagat and Durga Bhabhi's train reached Lucknow, he sent out a telegram to Bhagwati Charan: he would soon reach Calcutta with 'Durgawati'. The message startled Vohra. 'Who is Durgawati?' he wondered. When the trio reached Calcutta finally, Bhagwati Charan was surprised, and proud of Durga Devi. It was a perfect escape. 'Now I know that I am blessed with a true revolutionary as my partner,' Bhagwati Charan said.

There was some relief from the hawk-eyed

police at Lahore. But Calcutta was not 'safe' either. Over the next few days, Bhagwati Charan, Durga Devi and Bhagat Singh attended many important meetings in Calcutta. Later, Durga Devi returned to Lahore with Sachi. Bhagat had to remain underground for some more time.

~

It was time to meet an old friend. Bhagat met Batukeswar Dutt in Calcutta again. After the Kakori robbery and the string of arrests, Dutt had moved to Bihar and then to Calcutta. He worked with peasants and labourers. As he was fluent in Hindi, Batukeswar Dutt worked comfortably with migrant workers—helping them in their trade union work and fighting for their various demands.

Bhagat decided to leave Calcutta. The police were sharp and thanks to the rise in revolutionary activities in Bengal, the cops were always suspicious and conducting raids. Spies were everywhere. The HSRA leadership felt that Bhagat Singh's next destination could be Batukeswar Dutt's home in Oadi village. It was the ancestral house of the family, with several rooms in which he could easily remain hidden for a while.

The house was surrounded by trees and agricultural fields and hidden from prying eyes. But in a small village, people knew each other and the presence of a visitor could raise suspicion. Then Dutt had an idea. A relative's home had an underground room and Bhagat could well hide there for some days without anyone even spotting him! In the middle of the night, through serpentine roads, amid the croaking of frogs, Bhagat and Batukeswar moved from one house straight to the secret, underground room in the other house.

The duo lived here for the next two weeks. Sitting in the secret room, they would try to figure out what to do next. Something dramatic had to be planned that would make everyone notice. It had to be an action that could make millions of Indians understand the true purpose of the revolutionaries.

Chapter Eleven

The HSRA had its bomb-making dens in many cities in north India like Agra, Lahore, Saharanpur, Rohtak, and so on. Jatindranath Das, who was part of the Anushilan Samiti, was trained in bomb-making. Bhagat and Jatin often tested bombs together. Tests were sometimes conducted by the banks of River Ravi. It was a risky affair. Their secret could be out when blue smoke puffed up into the air or the strong odour from the laboratory spread to the surroundings. And yet they took it up most gladly—it had to be done for the country's freedom.

HSRA had a small office in Agra's Hing Ki Mandi. Though the space was for meetings, preparing pamphlets, posters, writing letters and so on, Bhagat had set up a library there with nearly two hundred books, mostly collected from friends and associates. There were books on economics, politics, the Russian Revolution, trade union movements and so on. He never wasted a moment. Even when he was actually 'underground', Bhagat did not stop reading.

Some months had passed since the assassination of Saunders, the train journey to Calcutta from Lahore, and hiding in Batukeswar Dutt's ancestral village home.

The British government, meanwhile, had brought two bills—the Public Safety Bill and the Trade Disputes Bill, which they wanted to pass as law. There was major opposition to these bills, which were thought to be 'anti-people'. The HSRA's Central Committee decided to oppose the bills.

It must be something spectacular that would draw the attention of the entire nation.

'We can throw bombs at the Central Assembly.'

'But we don't want to kill anyone.'

'It need not kill anyone, we will create fear among the British government.'

'It must be a strong act of protest, something in the lines of what French anarchist Vaillant did.'

'Ah yes, it must be something so loud that it can make even the deaf hear.'

Yes, they all agreed.

HSRA's decision was to keep Bhagat Singh out

of this and other revolutionaries were chosen for the job. *'If Bhagat courts arrest, it may eventually lead to trial in the Saunders murder case. We can't let him go right now. HSRA needs him.'*

HSRA leaders thought that Bhagat Singh could be sent to the Soviet Union.

But Sukhdev wanted Bhagat Singh to be in the operation. He knew that if anyone could make the deaf hear, it was Bhagat Singh. Some of their comrades felt that Sukhdev deliberately wanted to 'sacrifice' Bhagat. But others reasoned that Sukhdev was a perfect team leader, aware of the strengths and weaknesses of every comrade and had thus chosen Bhagat for the job. Only Bhagat can present the views of the revolutionaries to the world, he said.

The Central Committee met again, and finally

agreed to send Bhagat Singh and Batukeswar Dutt for the job.

~

At the HSRA's Sitaram Bazar den of Delhi, Bhagat Singh was busy writing the draft text of the leaflet. It started with the famous line by Vaillant: 'It takes a loud voice to make the deaf hear.' About forty copies were typed on the party's letterhead.

> Auguste Vaillant was a French anarchist who threw bombs at the French Chamber of Deputies on 9 December 1893. During his trial, Vaillant had said his purpose was not to kill but to wound the Deputies and the entire attack was planned in order to avenge the death of French anarchist Ravachol, who had been guillotined. Vaillant, too, was sentenced to death and killed by guillotine.

Bhagat Singh and Batukeswar Dutt were to strike on 8 April 1929. But first, there was going to be a picnic at Qudsia Bagh. Durga Devi and her sister-in-law Sushila had reached Delhi from Lahore. Chandrashekhar Azad and Bhagwati Charan Vohra were there, too, along with Bhagat. Durga and Sushila had got Bhagat's favourite food cooked. There were sweets and fruits. There was some laughter, someone cracked a joke, little Sachi was happy too, but all of them knew that Bhagat was going on a major operation, and they may lose him forever. But it would be for the freedom of the motherland.

Sachi had a lot of fun running around and playing with Lamba Chacha, his favourite uncle, Bhagat Singh. Before he was to leave, Sushila cut her thumb. With the blood, she made a tika and put it on Bhagat's forehead. It was meant to wish him well in the mission and to protect him from danger. Bhagat bade them farewell and headed straight to the Central Assembly. He and Batukeswar had studied the layout–the entrance, exit, and the routes that they should take. Bombs hidden under their clothes, the duo barged into the hall. Leaders of the Assembly like Mohammed Ali Jinnah and Madan Mohan Malviya were present when they got in.

The two hurled their bombs at the empty seats, which exploded immediately. Guns in hand, Bhagat and Batukeswar shouted slogans '*Inquilab Zindabaad*' and '*Samrajyavaad ka naash karo*' (Down with imperialism). They threw copies of the pamphlet 'To make the deaf hear'. There was chaos and confusion all around—some tried to run, others hid under tables. The leaders and the police were equally flabbergasted.

Bhagat and Batukeswar had prepared a meticulous plan. They had not gone there to run away after the 'action', so the question of fleeing did not arise.

'We have not come to harm anyone,' the duo shouted.

'We have come to make the deaf hear,' they said.

Saying this, they placed their guns on a table, as if they were surrendering. They were arrested immediately.

Meanwhile, outside the Central Assembly were Bhagat Singh's friends in a hired tonga. Bhagwati Charan Vohra, Durga Devi and Sushila were in the tonga with Sachi.

Soon, some figures emerged from the Central Assembly. From far, they spotted Bhagat and Batukeswar being taken away by the police. Little Sachinanda recognized Bhagat Singh even from far and called out, excitedly: 'Lamba Chacha!' For a moment, it seemed that Bhagat had looked up and caught a quick glimpse of the boy. The police, however, were too busy and did not notice the tonga.

The HSRA leaders were well prepared. Their statements promptly reached journalists. It began with Vaillant's lines: 'It takes a loud voice to make the deaf hear.'

HSRA officially announced that it was 'strongly justifying' the action of the Central

Assembly. Their statement was published in *The Hindustan Times* in its special evening edition the same day, 8 April 1929.

... Let the representatives of the people return to their constituencies and prepare the masses for the coming revolution. And let the Government know that, while protesting against the Public Safety and the Trades Disputes Bills and the callous murder of Lala Lajpat Rai on behalf of the helpless Indian masses, we want to emphasise the lesson often repeated by history that it is easy to kill the individuals, but you cannot kill ideas. Great empires crumbled but the ideas survived... We are sorry to admit that we who attach so great a sanctity to human life, we who dream of a glorious future when man will be enjoying perfect peace and full liberty, have been forced to shed human blood. But the sacrifice of the individuals

at the altar of the great revolution that will bring freedom to all rendering the exploitation of man by man impossible, is inevitable.

Long Live Revolution!

Chapter Twelve

Over the next few months, the police began to close in on the revolutionaries. In Lahore, HSRA's bomb factory was found in Kashmir House, which had been rented in the name of Bhagwati Charan Vohra. He was away during the raid. Though not arrested, Vohra had to go into hiding. Many others were arrested, including Sukhdev.

For Bhagat Singh, it was the beginning of a long period of serving his 'purpose' in jail. What was this purpose? It was for people across the country to awaken and take notice. And they did!

Very soon, it came to light that Bhagat Singh was part of the Saunders assassination.

The trial of the case, that came to be known as the Lahore Conspiracy Case, started on 10 July 1929. Bhagat and the others were charged with conspiracy to murder Scott and waging war against the King of England.

Bhagat was taken to Lahore, where he was beaten up brutally in prison. Undeterred, he continued to inspire the youth across the country in various ways. To the Second Punjab Students' Conference (whose president was Netaji Subhas Chandra Bose) at Lahore on 19 October 1929, Bhagat Singh and Batukeswar Dutt sent a message. It was read out at the open session:

'Today, we cannot ask the youth to take to pistols and bombs. Today, students are confronted with a far more important assignment... the youth will have to bear a great burden in this difficult time in the history of the nation... [they] will have to spread this revolutionary message... awaken crores of slum dwellers of the industrial areas and villagers living in worn-out cottages, so that we will be independent and the exploitation of man by man will become an impossibility...'

The hall reverberated with thunderous applause and cries of 'Bhagat Singh zindabad!'

During the trial, Bhagat Singh and the others would enter the courtroom raising slogans and singing revolutionary songs. Bhagat observed Lenin Day (on Lenin's death anniversary,

January 21), in the court. On 21 January 1930, he wore a red scarf to court, raising slogans of 'Long live Socialist Revolution', 'Long live Communist International', 'Lenin's name will never die'. He read out a telegram and asked the magistrate to send it to the Communist International or Comintern, an association of national communist parties founded in 1919. This is what it read: 'On Lenin Day we send hearty greetings to all who are doing something for carrying forward the ideas of the great Lenin. We wish success to the great experiment Russia is carrying out.'

Bhagat Singh had been 'invited' by none other than the Soviet leader, Joseph Stalin to visit the Soviet Union. The message didn't reach him eventually, and many wonder how it may have changed the course of Indian history if he had indeed travelled and met Stalin.

~

Meanwhile, Bhagat kept reading books in prison. It was as if he had very little time and his thirst for knowledge was endless. He kept a diary, in which he would jot down passages that he liked or felt relevant to his purpose.

Some of the notes he had jotted down were writings by Karl Marx, Vladimir Lenin, Friedrich Engels, Leon Trotsky, Bertrand Russel, Tommasso Campanella, Fyodor Dostoevsky, Jean Jacques Rousseau, and so on. He also loved reading fiction.

Bhagat Singh and Batukeswar Dutt were given life sentence for the Assembly bomb case.

Batukeswar Dutt was deported to the Andaman Cellular Jail, but the Saunders trial, in which Bhagat was involved, continued.

In prison, Bhagat pointed out the unfair discrimination between European and Indian prisoners, and he protested the miserable condition in which the latter had been lodged. Many political prisoners went on a hunger strike, demanding better food, clothes, hygienic conditions, access to books and newspapers.

The government felt more pressured as public support grew around their demands in prison. The jail authorities tried to force-feed them, but nothing worked.

Jatindra Nath Das was on hunger strike and his condition had deteriorated. Das died in September 1929 after sixty-three days of hunger strike. This created a great stir across the country and anger spread. There was a buzz across the country as the ideals of the young revolutionaries were discussed and debated everywhere. Their courage in fighting against the British was getting known everywhere and they were gaining in popularity. Bhagat Singh ended his hunger strike eventually. By then, he had moved millions of Indians to tears, becoming a household name in many parts of the country.

After many ups and downs in the trial, in May 1930, the British government decided to set up a special tribunal of three High Court judges. The tribunal gave its verdict on 7 October 1930: Bhagat Singh, Sukhdev Thapar and Shivaram Rajguru were to be hanged to death.

Jai Gopal had turned government approver in

the case along with Hans Raj Vohra, Phonindra Nath Ghosh and Manmohan Bannerji by giving statements against the trio. They were among the nearly 600 witnesses produced by the police in the case. Among the other accused, three were acquitted—Ajoy Ghosh, Jatindra Nath Sanyal and Des Raj. Many others got rigorous imprisonment and/or transportation for life.

~

When the trial was in the final stage, Bhagat Singh's father Kishan Singh wrote an appeal to the tribunal to say that his son had nothing to do with Saunders' murder and he must be given the opportunity to prove his innocence.

Bhagat was furious. He wrote a letter to his father on 4 October 1930.

> It has upset the whole equilibrium of my mind. In spite of all the sentiments and feelings of a father, I don't think you were... entitled to make such a move on my behalf without even consulting me...
>
> I feel as though I have been stabbed at the back. Had any other person done it, I would have considered it to be nothing short of treachery. But in your case, let me say that it has been a weakness—a weakness of the worst type.

I had only one idea before me throughout the trial, that is, to show complete indifference towards the trial in spite of the serious nature of the charges against us. I have always been of the opinion that all the political workers should be indifferent and should never bother about the legal fight in the law courts and should boldly bear the heaviest possible sentences inflicted upon them.

My life is not so precious, at least to me… It is not at all worth buying at the cost of my principles. There are other comrades of mine whose case is as serious as that of mine. We had adopted a common policy and we shall stand to the last, no matter how dearly we have to pay individually for it.

It is incredible that a person so young could be so strong, selfless and ready to embrace death.

Chapter Thirteen

One of the most inspiring aspects of Bhagat Singh's personality was his strength of character—firm, unbending and uncompromising in his principles. The essay 'Why I Am an Atheist' that he wrote while in prison, offers a great insight into his mental strength.

'I deny the very existence of that Almighty Supreme Being,' he wrote. Despite prodded by many to pray, Bhagat Singh did not do so till his last breath. He explained it all in his own writing while waiting to be hanged.

In his younger days, he did pray, due to the influence of his grandfather. During his school days, when he stayed in a boarding house for a year, apart from morning and evening prayers, he used to recite the Gayatri Mantra for hours. 'I was a perfect devotee in those days,' he wrote. His father, not orthodox in religion and who taught Bhagat the importance of the country's freedom, was also a believer in god. He encouraged Bhagat to pray daily.

While in National College, he 'began to think liberally and discuss and criticise all the religious problems, even about God', though he still believed in the existence of that entity. After joining the revolutionary party, he found that its leaders were believers too. 'All four Kakori martyrs passed their last days in prayers,' observed Bhagat.

But he learned to move away from prayers and faith in an unknown, invisible force, and formed his own path through his own reading and understanding. 'Study to arm yourself with arguments in favour of your cult. My previous faith and convictions underwent a remarkable modification...' he wrote. With his constant study of revolutionaries like Bakunin, Marx, Lenin, Trotsky and others, he found the common thread that they were all atheists.

'By the end of 1926 I had been convinced as to the baselessness of the theory of existence of an almighty supreme being who created, guided and controlled the universe,' he wrote.

When he was arrested in Lahore in May 1927, he refused to pray to draw strength. 'That was the real test and I came out successful... I was a staunch disbeliever and have ever since been... In God man can find very strong consolation and support. Without Him man has to depend upon himself. To stand upon one's own legs amid storms and hurricanes is not a child's play.'

And he was convinced that if more people became non-believers, it could lead to true liberty. 'The day we find a great number of men and women with this psychology... that day shall inaugurate the era of liberty.'

Bhagat's wish for an equal society found the existence of god unjustifiable. 'Why does your omnipotent God not stop every man when he is committing any sin or offence? ... Why does he not just produce a certain sentiment in the mind of the British people to liberate India? Why does he not infuse the altruistic enthusiasm in the hearts of all capitalists to forego their rights of personal possessions of means of production...?'

He reasoned that the capitalists were oppressing the poor and god was not intervening simply because there is no god. He blamed man for the suffering of other men which many passed off as the will of god.

British rule is here not because God wills it, but because they possess power and we do not dare to oppose them. Not that it is with the help of God that they are keeping us under their subjection, but it is with the help of guns and rifles, bomb and bullets, police and militia, and our apathy, that they are successfully committing the most deplorable sin against society—the outrageous exploitation of one nation by another.

Bhagat explained his views with clarity and logic. He had reached his philosophy through exhaustive reading. Bhagat was so convinced that he was willing to test his strength to prove himself right. 'I have read of atheists facing all troubles quite boldly; so I am trying to stand like a man with an erect head to the last, even on the gallows.'

~

After the judgment in which Bhagat Singh was sentenced to be hanged was delivered, he was perhaps the only person 'anxiously waiting' for his death. He wrote to Batukeswar Dutt in November 1930: 'In these cells, besides myself, there are many other prisoners who are waiting to be hanged. The only prayer of these people is that somehow or other they may escape the noose. Perhaps I am the only man amongst them who is anxiously waiting for the day when I will be fortunate enough to embrace the gallows for my ideal. I will climb the gallows gladly and show to the world as to how bravely the revolutionaries can sacrifice themselves for the cause.'

His writings show the glimpse of an individual who was so full of wisdom at such a young age.

All three waiting to be hanged showed a rare bravado before the enormous force of the British administration. They were brash, bold and full of relentless arrogance against the colonizers. This fearlessness reflected in their letter to the Punjab Governor, in which Bhagat, Sukhdev and Rajguru wrote: 'No hanging, please shoot us.'

They wrote: 'According to the verdict of your

court we had waged war and we are therefore war prisoners. And we claim to be treated as such.' Their letter said that the government was trying to win over leaders of 'the upper strata of the Indian society through petty concessions and compromises'. But, according to them, their firm belief was that 'the days of capitalist and imperialist exploitation are numbered.'

They were sentenced to death and ordered to be hanged on 24 March 1931, but the schedule was changed and they were hanged a day earlier, on 23 March at 7.30 p.m. at Lahore Central Jail. Usually death by hanging is conducted at dawn but the British police apprehended trouble. The Naujawan Bharat Sabha had organized a rally and emotions were running high.

There are many stories on Bhagat Singh's last

moments. All of them say that he refused to pray, he was an atheist and wanted to remain so till his dying moment.

A story narrated by his close associate Manmathnath Gupta mentions that when he was called upon to mount the scaffold, Bhagat Singh was reading a book either written by Lenin or on Lenin. He continued reading and said: 'Wait a while. A revolutionary is talking to another revolutionary.' After a few moments, he flung the book towards the ceiling and said, 'Let us go.'

There is another story that said that a few hours before he was hanged, Bhagat Singh's lawyer Prem Nath Mehta met him and asked him his message for the nation. 'Down with Imperialism!' and 'Long Live Revolution' was his answer. He added that he wished to be born again in the same country so he could serve India again.

Other narratives mention that all the three revolutionaries sang:

Kabhi woh din bhi ayega ke jab azad hum honge
Yeh apni hi zameen hogi yeh apna asmaan hoga
Shahidon ki chitaon par lagenge har baar mele
Watan par marne walon ka yehi nam-o-nishan hoga

(Someday that day will come when we will be free / This will be our land and this our sky / People will gather on the grounds where once / Martyrs' pyres were lit / A tribute to all those who / Gave their lives for their land)

The bodies of the three martyrs were taken away secretly from the prison. The families did not get a chance to perform the last rites. In this too, the British showed brutality. But the news of the hanging had spread. People located a spot, and suspecting that the British had tried to bury them there, the followers of Bhagat Singh and the other revolutionaries collected some soil from the spot and cremated that by the banks of the river Ravi.

~

After the martyrs had sacrificed their lives, Gandhiji faced angry youths who showed him black flags when he reached Karachi for the Congress party's annual convention. The matter was taken up by Jawaharlal Nehru and Madan Mohan Malviya, and the Congress placed on record its admiration of the bravery and sacrifice of Bhagat Singh, Sukhdev and Rajguru. They added that 'the [British] Government had lost a golden opportunity for promoting goodwill between the two nations.'

Some allege that Gandhiji should have done more to save Bhagat Singh, Sukhdev and Rajguru from the gallows. But others say that he did raise the matter with Lord Irwin, the Viceroy of India, with whom he was in talks for some time.

Was Bhagat Singh's trial and hanging a 'judicial murder' as some say?

It is said that the case against Bhagat Singh was flawed, as the FIR did not contain his name in the Saunders murder but had the mention of 'two unidentified' men as accused. It was only after the trial in the bomb case that the British police connected him with the Saunders assassination. The death warrant was alleged to be illegal. Many more flaws in the entire trial have been pointed out by legal experts. Several legal steps followed to counter the verdict of execution, but it seemed that the British government was bent upon executing them. The friends of Bhagat Singh who had turned government approvers, including Jai Gopal, were all rewarded by the police.

~

Bhagat Singh was in jail for about two years from 8 April 1929 to 23 March 1931. It is said that he had written some books during this time, which he had handed over to someone. But these got misplaced or were perhaps destroyed. Some of his writings, including his jail diary and some essays and letters, have survived, but most are feared to have been destroyed and lost forever.

But the idea of Bhagat Singh lives. He was

a rare young man whose life was over at just twenty-four years. He was an unusual mix of strength and softness. His decisions and ideals were guided both by gentle affection and sympathy for those who suffer, as well as a strong will to make a difference to the world even at the cost of his own life. He was guided by the will to work for the poor, for peasants and workers, and to empower them. His idea of freedom was that true power should be with the common people.

It was impossible to sway him from his position once he had taken a stand. For generations, Bhagat Singh has remained a youth icon and a great example of courage, boldness of action, and strength of character. He is, undoubtedly, one of the greatest freedom fighters of India.

It is however, important to remember that

Bhagat Singh's actions are not beyond criticism. Some look at him as a controversial figure. The method he adopted—violence—would not be justifiable or reasonable to all. It is imperative to read his story as told in this book, not as an attempt to valorise him, but one that tries to bring out his passion, dedication and the way he was true to his thoughts and beliefs.

Bhagat Singh: *A Timeline*

- 27 September 1907: Bhagat Singh is born in Banga of Lyallpur in Punjab province, now in Pakistan.
- 13 April 1919: Jallianwala Bagh massacre takes place in Amritsar, Punjab.
- November 1915: Kartar Singh Sarabha, a nineteen-year-old Ghadarite, is hanged by the British.
- 4 February 1922: The Chauri-Chaura incident in which three civilians and twenty-three policemen die occurs.

- February 1922: Mahatma Gandhi calls off the Non-cooperation movement.
- 1923: Bhagat Singh starts writing for various newspapers and magazines.
- October 1924: Hindustan Republican Association (HRA) is formed.
- 9 August 1925: The Kakori train robbery is carried out by HRA members.
- 1926: Naujawan Bharat Sabha (NBS) is formed, influenced by youth organizations in Italy. Bhagat Singh is its general secretary.
- May 1927: Bhagat Singh is arrested in Lahore, and released later against a bond of Rs 60,000.
- November 1927: Simon Commission is formed.
- September 1928: HRA's name changed to Hindustan Socialist Republican Association

(HRSA). Bhagat Singh becomes a top functionary.

- 30 October 1928: Lala Lajpat Rai injured by the police during protests against the Simon Commission.
- 17 November 1928: Lala Lajpat Rai dies.
- 17 December 1928: Assistant Police Superintendent J.P. Saunders killed by HSRA activists.
- 8 April 1929: Bombs hurled in the Central Assembly in Delhi by Bhagat Singh and Batukeswar Dutt.
- 7 October 1930: Bhagat Singh, Shivaram Rajguru and Sukhdev Thapar are sentenced to death.
- 23 March 1931: Bhagat Singh is hanged along with Sukhdev Thapar and Shivaram Rajguru.

Author's Note

When parents get too protective about their children or people are doubtful about the abilities of young persons, it is good to remember what Bhagat Singh had achieved at such a young age. His fearlessness, distinctive thought process, unique politics, unbending character, his love of reading were awe-inspiring.

I relied on *Bhagat Singh: The Jail Notebook and Other Writings,* Compiled with an Introduction by Chaman Lal (the Jail Notebook annotated by Bhupender Hooja), published by

LeftWord Books, New Delhi, 2007. I also read several pieces written by Chaman Lal, who is an expert on Bhagat Singh.

Lahore University of Management Studies (LUMS) digital archive website helped me get details on letters, photographs, maps, notices, etc., related to Bhagat Singh. I also read hundreds of newspaper articles, editorials and book excerpts on him. Some of these are: excerpt in Scroll.in from Kama Maclean's *A Revolutionary History of Interwar India: Violence, Image, Voice and Text*, Penguin Books, 2016; the article, 'Khatkar Kalan is Bhagat Singh's ancestral village but he never lived there,' published by PTI, 23 March 2022 (archive.ptinews.com); 'Revolution to ruins: the tragic fall of Bradlaugh Hall', by Aown Ali, published in Dawn.com, 26 September 2015; 'The library that shaped Bhagat Singh and the Indian

Revolutionary Movement', by Harshvardhan, published in thewire.in on 28 September 2022. Some other articles are: 'Towards Independence and Socialist Republic: Naujawan Bharat Sabha', by S.K. Mittal and Irfan Habib, published in *Social Scientist*, Vol. 8, No. 2 (Sept 1979), 'The Lone Ranger: Ganesh Shankar Vidyarthi and His Crusade Against Communalism, from 1915 to 1931', by P.K. Shukla, from *Proceedings of the Indian History Congress*, Vol. 64 (2003) pp 1026-1035, published in JSTOR.

I would like to thank Sudeshna Shome Ghosh for giving me this wonderful opportunity to get to know so many facets of Bhagat Singh. Thank you Sudeshna and Radhika Shenoy for the editing, and Sridatri Tagore for the illustrations.

Swati Sengupta